Dynamic Quilt
Designs
made simple

LEISURE ARTS, INC.
Little Rock, Arkansas

D1560766

HAVE FUN DISCOVERING

how diamonds, rectangles, and squares are easily sewn into (seemingly complex!) visual delights. The simple fabric shapes come together to create a series of six exciting quilts in this new collection by Sue Harvey and Sandy Boobar. The patterns include four generous throws, one quilt for a twin-size bed, and one for a queen-size bed. Choose fabrics with plenty of contrast to make these pleasing geometric designs!

EDITORIAL STAFF

Vice President of Editorial:
Susan White Sullivan
Special Projects Director: Susan Frantz Wiles
Director of E-Commerce and
Prepress Services: Mark Hawkins
Art Publications Director: Rhonda Shelby
Technical Editor: Lisa Lancaster
Technical Writer: Frances Huddleston
Technical Associates: Mary Hutcheson
and Jean Lewis
Editorial Writer: Susan McManus Johnson
Art Category Manager: Lora Puls
Graphic Artists: Stacy Owens and
Becca Snider Tally
Imaging Technician: Stephanie Johnson
Prepress Technician: Janie Marie Wright
Photography Manager: Katherine Laughlin
Contributing Photographer: Mark Mathews
Contributing Photo Stylist: Christy Myers
Manager of E-Commerce: Robert Young

BUSINESS STAFF

President and Chief Executive Officer:
Rick Barton
Vice President of Sales: Mike Behar
Vice President of Finance:
Laticia Mull Dittrich
Director of Corporate Planning:
Anne Martin
National Sales Director: Martha Adams
Information Technology Director:
Brian Roden
Controller: Francis Caple
Vice President of Operations: Jim Dittrich
Retail Customer Service Manager:
Stan Raynor
Vice President of Purchasing: Fred F. Pruss

Made in China.

Library of Congress Control Number: 2012937449

ISBN-13: 978-1-4647-0263-1

AUTUMN VIEW

Finished Quilt Size: 69³/₄" x 87³/₄" (177 cm x 223 cm)
Finished Block Size: 8" x 8" (20 cm x 20 cm)

WHAT YOU WILL NEED

Yardage is based on 43"/44" (109 cm/112 cm) wide fabric with a usable width of 40" (102 cm).

- 3 yds (2.7 m) of dark green print fabric
- ¹/₈ yd (11 cm) of dark green tonal fabric
- ¹/₄ yd (23 cm) of medium green tonal fabric
- 1¹/₂ yds (1.4 m) of rust print fabric
- 1³/₈ yds (1.3 m) of tan print fabric
- ³/₈ yd (34 cm) of tan tonal fabric
- ⁵/₈ yd (57 cm) of purple print fabric
- ⁵/₈ yd (57 cm) of fabric for binding
- 5³/₈ yds (4.9 m) of fabric for backing

You will also need:

- 78" x 96" (198 cm x 244 cm) piece of batting

CUTTING THE PIECES

*Follow **Rotary Cutting**, page 54, to cut fabric. Cut all strips from the selvage-to-selvage width of the fabric. All measurements include ¹/₄" seam allowances.*

From dark green print fabric:
- Cut 8 outer border strips 6¹/₂" wide.
- Cut 9 strips 5" wide. From these strips, cut 72 squares 5" x 5".

From dark green tonal fabric:
- Cut 2 strips 1¹/₂" wide. From these strips, cut 35 sashing squares 1¹/₂" x 1¹/₂".

From medium green tonal fabric:
- Cut 3 strips 2¹/₂" wide.

From rust print fabric:
- Cut 7 inner border strips 2¹/₂" wide.
- Cut 21 strips 1¹/₂" wide. From these strips, cut 82 sashings 1¹/₂" x 8¹/₂".

From tan print fabric:
- Cut 6 strips 2¹/₂" wide.
- Cut 6 strips 5" wide. From these strips, cut 48 squares 5" x 5".

From tan tonal fabric:
- Cut 2 strips 5" wide. From these strips, cut 11 squares 5" x 5".

From purple print fabric:
- Cut 3 strips 2¹/₂" wide.
- Cut 2 strips 5" wide. From these strips, cut 13 squares 5" x 5".

From fabric for binding:
- Cut 9 binding strips 2¹/₄" wide.

MAKING THE FOUR-PATCHES

*Follow **Piecing**, page 55, and **Pressing**, page 56, to make quilt top.*

1. Sew 1 tan print **strip** and 1 medium green tonal **strip** together to make **Strip Set A**. Press seam allowances to green strip. Make 3 Strip Set A's. Cut across Strip Set A's at 2¹/₂" intervals to make 48 **Unit 1's**.

Strip Set A
(make 3)

Unit 1
(make 48)

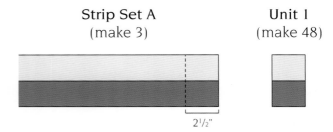

2¹/₂"

2. Sew 1 tan print **strip** and 1 purple print **strip** together to make **Strip Set B**. Press seam allowances to purple strip. Make 3 Strip Set B's. Cut across Strip Set B's at 2¹/₂" intervals to make 48 **Unit 2's**.

Strip Set B
(make 3)

Unit 2
(make 48)

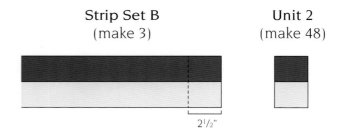

2¹/₂"

3. Sew 1 **Unit 1** and 1 **Unit 2** together to make **Four Patch**. Press seam allowances to one side. Four Patch should measure 4¹/₂" x 4¹/₂" including seam allowances. Make 48 Four Patches.

Four Patch (make 48)

MAKING THE TRIANGLE-SQUARES

1. Draw a diagonal line on wrong side of each tan print, tan tonal, and purple print **square**.
2. Matching right sides, place 1 tan print **square** on top of 1 dark green print **square**. Stitch ¹/₄" from each side of drawn line (**Fig. 1**). Cut along drawn line and press seam allowances to green print to make 2 **Triangle-Square A's**. Make 96 Triangle-Square A's. Trim each Triangle-Square A to 4¹/₂" x 4¹/₂".

Fig. 1

Triangle-Square A (make 96)

3. In the same manner, use purple print **squares** and dark green print **squares** to make 26 **Triangle-Square B's**. Press seam allowances to green print. Trim each Triangle-Square B to 4¹/₂" x 4¹/₂".

Triangle-Square B (make 26)

4. In the same manner, use tan tonal **squares** and dark green print **squares** to make 22 **Triangle-Square C's**. Press seam allowances to green print. Trim each Triangle-Square C to 4¹/₂" x 4¹/₂".

Triangle-Square C (make 22)

MAKING THE BLOCKS

1. Sew 1 **Four Patch** and 1 **Triangle-Square** A together to make **Unit 3**. Press seam allowances to Four Patch. Make 48 Unit 3's.

Unit 3 (make 48)

2. Sew 1 **Triangle-Square A** and 1 **Triangle-Square B** together to make **Unit 4**. Press seam allowances to Triangle-Square B. Make 26 Unit 4's.

Unit 4 (make 26)

3. Sew 1 **Triangle-Square A** and 1 **Triangle-Square C** together to make **Unit 5**. Press seam allowances to Triangle-Square C. Make 22 Unit 5's.

Unit 5 (make 22)

4. Sew 1 **Unit 3** and 1 **Unit 4** together to make **Block A**. Press seam allowances to one side. Block A should measure $8\frac{1}{2}$" x $8\frac{1}{2}$" including seam allowances. Make 26 Block A's.

Block A (make 26)

5. Sew 1 **Unit 3** and 1 **Unit 5** together to make **Block B**. Press seam allowances to one side. Block B should measure $8\frac{1}{2}$" x $8\frac{1}{2}$" including seam allowances. Make 22 Block B's.

Block B (make 22)

ASSEMBLING THE QUILT TOP CENTER

Refer to Quilt Top Diagram to assemble quilt top.
Pay special attention to Block A and B placement and orientation.

1. Sew 6 **Blocks** and 5 **sashings** together to make **Row**. Press seam allowances to sashings. Make 8 Rows.
2. Sew 6 **sashings** and 5 **sashing squares** together to make **Sashing Row**. Press seam allowances to sashings. Make 7 Sashing Rows.
3. Sew **Rows** and **Sashing Rows** together to complete quilt top center. Press seam allowances to Sashing Rows.

ADDING THE BORDERS

1. Sew **inner border strips** together, end to end, to make 1 continuous strip.
2. To determine length of side inner borders, measure *length* across center of quilt top center. Cut 2 **side inner borders** from continuous strip. Matching centers and corners, sew side inner borders to quilt top center. Press seam allowances to border.
3. To determine length of top/bottom inner borders, measure *width* across center of quilt top center (including added borders). Cut 2 **top/bottom inner borders** from continuous strip. Matching centers and corners, sew top/bottom borders to quilt top center. Press seam allowances to border.
4. In the same manner, use **outer borders strips** to add **side** and then **top/bottom outer borders** to quilt top. Press seam allowances to outer border.

COMPLETING THE QUILT

1. Follow **Quilting**, page 56, to mark, layer, and quilt as desired. Quilt shown is machine quilted with an all-over leaf pattern.
2. Follow **Making a Hanging Sleeve**, page 60, if a hanging sleeve is desired.
3. Use **binding strips** and follow **Binding**, page 60, to bind quilt.

Quilt Top Diagram

COOL
BLUE

Finished Quilt Size: 64³/₄" x 76³/₄" (164 cm x 195 cm)
Finished Block Size: 16" x 20" (41 cm x 51 cm)

WHAT YOU WILL NEED

Yardage is based on 43"/44" (109 cm/112 cm) wide fabric with a usable width of 40" (102 cm).

- 1¹/₂ yds (1.4 m) of large floral fabric (outer border)
- ⁵/₈ yd (57 cm) of cream leaf print fabric
- ⁵/₈ yd (57 cm) of cream paisley fabric
- ⁷/₈ yd (80 cm) of brown floral fabric
- 1³/₈ yds (1.3 m) of brown small print fabric
- 1¹/₄ yds (1.1 m) of light aqua print fabric
- 1¹/₈ yds (1 m) of dark aqua print fabric
- ⁵/₈ yd (57 cm) of fabric for binding
- 4³/₄ yds (4.3 m) of fabric for backing

You will also need:

- 73" x 85" (185 cm x 216 cm) piece of batting
- Spray starch

13

CUTTING THE PIECES

*Follow **Rotary Cutting**, page 54, to cut fabric. Cut all strips from the selvage-to-selvage width of the fabric. All measurements include ¼" seam allowances.*

From large floral fabric:
- Cut 7 **outer border strips** 6½" wide.

From cream leaf print fabric:
- Cut 5 strips 3½" wide. From these strips, cut 36 **rectangles E** 3½" x 4½".

From cream paisley fabric:
- Cut 2 strips 8½" wide. From these strips, cut 3 **rectangles F** 8½" x 14½".

From brown floral fabric:
- Cut 3 strips 8½" wide. From these strips, cut 6 **rectangles A** 8½" x 14½".

From brown small print fabric:
- Cut 12 strips 3¾" wide. From these strips, cut 72 **rectangles C** 3¾" x 6".

From light aqua print fabric:
- Cut 6 strips 4½" wide. From these strips, cut 12 **rectangles B** 4½" x 14½".
- Cut 3 strips 3½" wide. From these strips, cut 12 **rectangles D** 3½" x 8½".

From dark aqua print fabric:
- Cut 6 **inner border strips** 2½" wide.
- Cut 3 strips 4½" wide. From these strips, cut 6 **rectangles G** 4½" x 14½".
- Cut 2 strips 3½" wide. From these strips, cut 6 **rectangles H** 3½" x 8½".

From fabric for binding:
- Cut 8 **binding strips** 2¼" wide.

MAKING THE UNITS

*Follow **Piecing**, page 55, and **Pressing**, page 56, to make quilt top.*

1. With 1 **rectangle B** right side up, use pencil to make marks 4⅛" from corners on short edges and marks 3⅛" from same corners on 1 long edge as shown (**Fig. 1**). Draw lines between marks. Repeat for each **rectangle B** and **G**.

Fig. 1

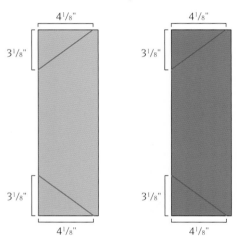

2. With 1 **rectangle D** right side up, make marks 3⅛" from corners on short edges and marks 4⅛" from same corners on 1 long edge as shown (**Fig. 2**). Draw lines between marks. Repeat for each **rectangle D** and **H**.

Fig. 2

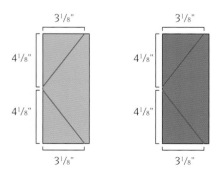

3. Apply spray starch to each **rectangle C** and press dry.

4. With right sides together and extending corner of rectangle C ¹/₄" beyond long edge of rectangle B, align long edge of 1 **rectangle C** with drawn line on 1 **rectangle B** (**Fig. 3**). Stitch ¹/₄" from edge of rectangle C.

Fig. 3

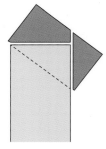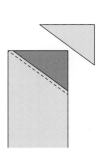

5. Press rectangle C to right side to cover corner of rectangle B. With wrong sides facing up, trim rectangle C even with edges of rectangle B (**Fig. 4**). Fold back remainder of rectangle C and trim corner of rectangle B, leaving a ¹/₄" seam allowance (**Fig. 5**).

Fig. 4   Fig. 5

6. In the same manner, sew a second **rectangle C** to opposite end of rectangle B to complete **Unit 1**.

7. Repeat Steps 4-6 to make a total of 12 Unit 1's.

Unit 1 (make 12)

8. Using **rectangles C** and **G**, repeat Steps 4-6 to make 6 **Unit 2's**.

Unit 2 (make 6)

9. In the same manner, use **rectangles C** and **D** to make 12 **Unit 3's**.

Unit 3 (make 12)

10. In the same manner, use **rectangles C** and **H** to make 6 **Unit 4's**.

Unit 4 (make 6)

MAKING THE BLOCKS

1. Sew 1 **Unit 3** and 2 **rectangles E** together to make **Unit 5**. Make 12 Unit 5's.

Unit 5 (make 12)

2. Sew 2 **Unit 1's** and 1 **rectangle A** together to make **Unit 6**. Make 6 Unit 6's.

Unit 6 (make 6)

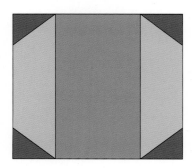

3. Sew 2 **Unit 5's** and 1 **Unit 6** together to make **Block A**. Block A should measure 16½" x 20½" including seam allowances. Make 6 Block A's.

Block A (make 6)

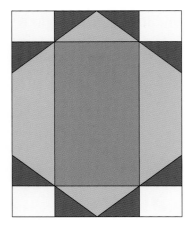

4. Sew 1 **Unit 4** and 2 **rectangles E** together to make **Unit 7**. Make 6 Unit 7's.

Unit 7 (make 6)

5. Sew 2 **Unit 2's** and 1 **rectangle F** together to make **Unit 8**. Make 3 Unit 8's.

Unit 8 (make 3)

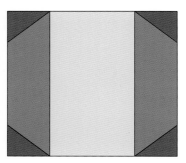

6. Sew 2 **Unit 7's** and 1 **Unit 8** together to make **Block B**. Block B should measure 16$\frac{1}{2}$" x 20$\frac{1}{2}$" including seam allowances. Make 3 Block B's.

Block B (make 3)

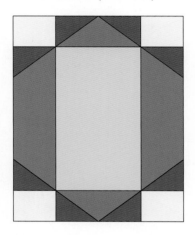

ASSEMBLING THE QUILT TOP CENTER

1. Sew 2 **Block A's** and 1 **Block B** together to make **Row**. Make 3 Rows.

Row (make 3)

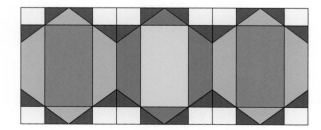

2. Referring to **Quilt Top Diagram**, sew **Rows** together to complete quilt top center.

ADDING THE BORDERS

1. Sew **inner border strips** together, end to end, to make 1 continuous strip.
2. To determine length of side inner borders, measure *length* across center of quilt top center. Cut 2 **side inner borders** from continuous strip. Matching centers and corners, sew side inner borders to quilt top center.
3. To determine length of top/bottom inner borders, measure *width* across center of quilt top center (including added borders). Cut 2 **top/bottom inner borders** from continuous strip. Matching centers and corners, sew top/bottom borders to quilt top center.
4. In the same manner, use **outer borders strips** to add **side** and then **top/bottom outer borders** to quilt top.

COMPLETING THE QUILT

1. Follow **Quilting**, page 56, to mark, layer, and quilt as desired. Quilt shown is machine quilted with a continuous flower and leaf pattern.
2. Follow **Making a Hanging Sleeve**, page 60, if a hanging sleeve is desired.
3. Use **binding strips** and follow **Binding**, page 60, to bind quilt.

Quilt Top Diagram

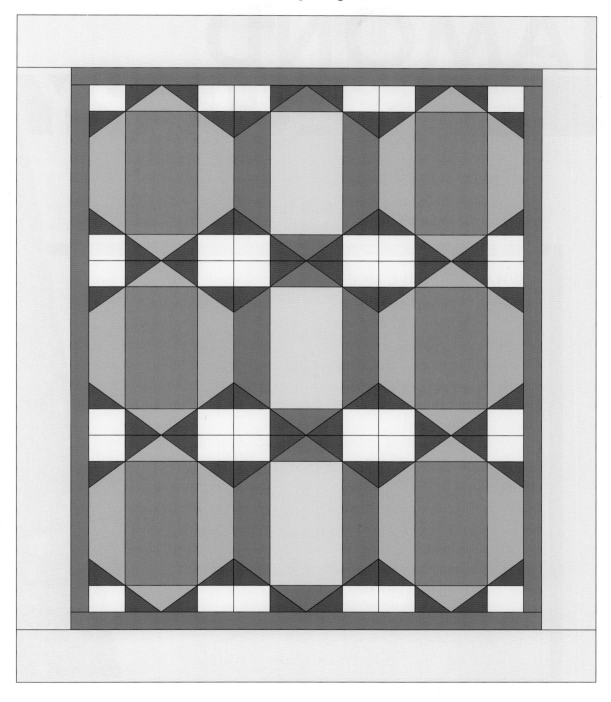

DIAMOND GALLERY

Finished Quilt Size: 64³/₄" x 76³/₄" (164 cm x 195 cm)
Finished Block Size: 12" x 12" (30 cm x 30 cm)

WHAT YOU WILL NEED

Yardage is based on 43"/44" (109 cm/112 cm) wide fabric with a usable width of 40" (102 cm).

- 1¹/₂ yds (1.4 cm) of navy floral fabric for outer border and block centers
- 1¹/₈ yds (1 m) of navy leaf print fabric for large rectangular shapes
- ³/₈ yd (34 cm) of light blue scroll print fabric for background
- ¹/₈ yd (11 cm) of pale blue print fabric for blocks
- 1¹/₄ yds (1.1 m) of olive print fabric for large rectangular shapes and blocks
- ³/₈ yd (34 cm) of yellow-green print fabric for blocks
- ³/₄ yd (69 cm) of navy/olive scroll print fabric for blocks
- 1³/₄ yds (1.6 m) of light blue/olive scroll print fabric for blocks
- 1¹/₈ yds (1 m) of black solid fabric for inner border and blocks
- ⁵/₈ yd (57 cm) of fabric for binding
- 4³/₄ yds (4.3 m) of fabric for backing

You will also need:

- 73" x 85" (185 cm x 216 cm) piece of batting

CUTTING THE PIECES

*Follow **Rotary Cutting**, page 54, to cut fabric. Cut all strips from the selvage-to-selvage width of the fabric. All measurements include 1/4" seam allowances.*

From navy floral fabric:
- Cut 7 outer border strips 6 1/2" wide.
- Cut 1 strip 3 1/2" wide. From this strip, cut 10 squares A 3 1/2" x 3 1/2".

From navy leaf print fabric:
- Cut 7 strips 4 1/2" wide. From these strips, cut 50 squares N 4 1/2" x 4 1/2".
- Cut 1 strip 5" wide. From this strip, cut 5 squares W 5" x 5".

From light blue scroll print fabric:
- Cut 2 strips F 2" wide.
- Cut 1 strip H 7" wide.

From pale blue print fabric:
- Cut 3 strips 1" wide. From this strip, cut 10 strips O 1" x 3 1/2" and 10 strips P 1" x 4 1/2".

From olive print fabric:
- Cut 3 strips 1" wide. From this strip, cut 10 strips B 1" x 3 1/2" and 10 strips C 1" x 4 1/2".
- Cut 5 strips 4 1/2" wide. From these strips, cut 40 squares S 4 1/2" x 4 1/2".
- Cut 3 strips 4 1/2" wide. From these strips, cut 10 rectangles V 4 1/2" x 8 1/2".

From yellow-green print fabric:
- Cut 2 strips Q 2" wide.
- Cut 1 strip R 7" wide.

From navy/olive scroll print fabric:
- Cut 4 strips G 2" wide.
- Cut 2 strips I 2" wide.
- Cut 5 strips 2" wide. From these strips, cut 20 rectangles J 2" x 8 1/2".

From light blue/olive scroll print fabric:
- Cut 2 strips 3 1/2" wide. From these strips, cut 20 squares K 3 1/2" x 3 1/2".
- Cut 8 strips 4 1/2" wide. From these strips, cut 30 rectangles T 4 1/2" x 8 1/2".
- Cut 2 strips 4 1/2" wide. From these strips, cut 10 squares U 4 1/2" x 4 1/2".
- Cut 1 strip 5" wide. From this strip, cut 5 squares X 5" x 5".

From black solid fabric:
- Cut 6 inner border strips 2 1/2" wide.
- Cut 20 strips 1" wide. From these strips, cut 20 strips D 1" x 4 1/2", 20 strips E 1" x 5 1/2", 20 strips L 1" x 11 1/2", and 20 strips M 1" x 12 1/2".

From fabric for binding:
- Cut 8 binding strips 2 1/4" wide.

CUTTING TIP

When there are many pieces, separate the pieces by letter in labeled zip bags or envelopes.

MAKING THE BLOCKS A AND B

*Follow **Piecing**, page 55, and **Pressing**, page 56, to make quilt top. Arrows on diagrams indicate direction to press seam allowances.*

1. Sew 2 **strips B** to opposite sides of 1 **square A** and then sew 2 **strips C** to remaining sides to make **Unit 1-A**. Make 5 Unit 1-A's.

   Sew 2 **strips O** to opposite sides of 1 **square A** and then sew 2 **strips P** to remaining sides to make **Unit 1-B**. Make 5 Unit 1-B's.

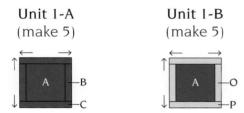

   Unit 1-A (make 5)   Unit 1-B (make 5)

2. Sew 2 **strips D** to opposite sides of 1 **Unit 1-A** and then sew 2 **strips E** to remaining sides to make **Unit 2-A**. Unit 2-A should measure 5¹/₂" x 5¹/₂" including seam allowances. Make 5 Unit 2-A's.

   Sew 2 **strips D** to opposite sides of 1 **Unit 1-B** and then sew 2 **strips E** to remaining sides to make **Unit 2-B**. Unit 2-B should measure 5¹/₂" x 5¹/₂" including seam allowances. Make 5 Unit 2-B's.

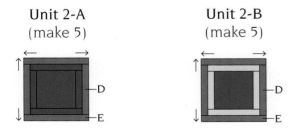

   Unit 2-A (make 5)   Unit 2-B (make 5)

3. Sew 1 **strip F** and 1 **strip G** together to make **Strip Set A**. Make 2 Strip Set A's. Cut across Strip Set A's at 5¹/₂" intervals to make 10 **Unit 3-A's**.

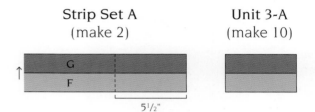

   Strip Set A (make 2)   Unit 3-A (make 10)

   Sew 1 **strip Q** and 1 **strip G** together to make **Strip Set B**. Make 2 Strip Set B's. Cut across Strip Set B's at 5¹/₂" intervals to make 10 **Unit 3-B's**.

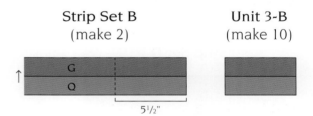

   Strip Set B (make 2)   Unit 3-B (make 10)

4. Sew 2 **Unit 3-A's** and 1 **Unit 2-A** together to make **Unit 4-A**. Unit 4-A should measure 11¹/₂" x 5¹/₂" including seam allowances. Make 5 Unit 4-A's.

   Sew 2 **Unit 3-B's** and 1 **Unit 2-B** together to make **Unit 4-B**. Unit 4-B should measure 11¹/₂" x 5¹/₂" including seam allowances. Make 5 Unit 4-B's.

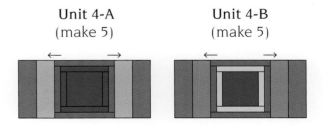

   Unit 4-A (make 5)   Unit 4-B (make 5)

5. Sew 1 **strip H** and 1 **strip I** together to make **Strip Set C**. Cut across Strip Set C at 2" intervals to make 10 **Unit 5-A's**.

Strip Set C

Unit 5-A
(make 10)

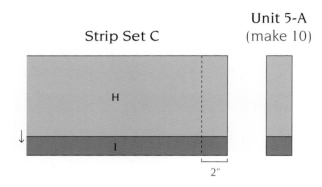

Sew 1 **strip R** and 1 **strip I** together to make **Strip Set D**. Cut across Strip Set D at 2" intervals to make 10 **Unit 5-B's**.

Strip Set D

Unit 5-B
(make 10)

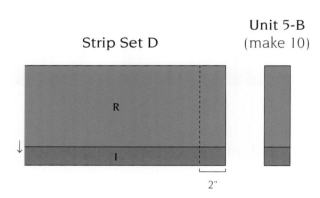

6. Sew 1 **Unit 5-A** and 1 **strip J** together to make **Unit 6-A**. Make 10 Unit 6-A's.

Sew 1 **Unit 5-B** and 1 **strip J** together to make **Unit 6-B**. Make 10 Unit 6-B's.

Unit 6-A
(make 10)

Unit 6-B
(make 10)

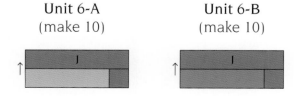

7. Sew 1 **Unit 6-A** and 1 **square K** together to make **Unit 7-A**. Unit 7-A should measure 11½" x 3½" including seam allowances. Make 10 Unit 7-A's.

Sew 1 **Unit 6-B** and 1 **square K** together to make **Unit 7-B**. Unit 7-B should measure 11½" x 3½" including seam allowances. Make 10 Unit 7-B's.

Unit 7-A
(make 10)

Unit 7-B
(make 10)

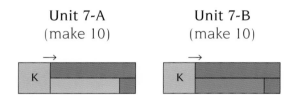

8. Sew 2 **Unit 7-A's** and 1 **Unit 4-A** together to make **Unit 8-A**. Unit 8-A should measure 11½" x 11½" including seam allowances. Make 5 Unit 8-A's.

Sew 2 **Unit 7-B's** and 1 **Unit 4-B** together to make **Unit 8-B**. Unit 8-B should measure 11½" x 11½" including seam allowances. Make 5 Unit 8-B's.

Unit 8-A
(make 5)

Unit 8-B
(make 5)

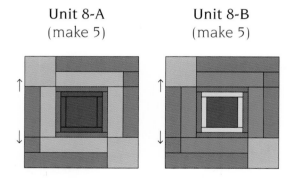

9.   Sew 2 **strips L** to opposite sides of 1 **Unit 8-A** and then sew 2 **strips M** to remaining sides to make **Unit 9-A**. Make 5 Unit 9-A's.

Sew 2 **strips L** to opposite sides of 1 **Unit 8-B** and then sew 2 **strips M** to remaining sides to make **Unit 9-B**. Make 5 Unit 9-B's.

Unit 9-A
(make 5)

Unit 9-B
(make 5)

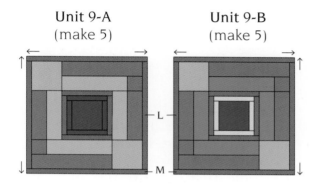

10. Draw a diagonal line on wrong side of each **square N** and **square S**.

11. With right sides together, place 2 **square N's** on opposite corners of 1 **Unit 9-A**. Stitch along drawn lines (**Fig. 1**). Trim ¹/₄" from stitching line and press open to make **Block A**. Block A should measure 12¹/₂" x 12¹/₂" including seam allowances. Make 5 Block A's.

In the same manner, add 2 **squares S** to opposite corners of each **Unit 9-B** to make 5 **Block B's**. Block B should measure 12¹/₂" x 12¹/₂" including seam allowances.

Fig. 1

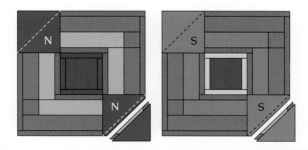

Block A
(make 5)

Block B
(make 5)

MAKING THE BLOCKS C AND D

1.   Draw a diagonal line on wrong side of each **square U** and **square X**.

2.   Matching right sides, place 1 **square X** on top of 1 **square W**. Stitch ¹/₄" from each side of drawn line (**Fig. 2**). Cut along drawn line and press to darker fabric to make 2 **Triangle-Squares**. Make 10 Triangle-Squares. Trim each Triangle-Square to 4¹/₂" x 4¹/₂".

Fig. 2

Triangle-Square (make 10)

3. Matching right sides, place 1 **square N** on left end of 1 **rectangle T** and stitch along drawn line. Trim ¼" from stitching line (**Fig. 3**); press open (**Fig. 4**).

Fig. 3

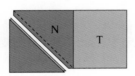

Fig. 4

4. Place 1 **square S** on opposite end of **rectangle T**. Stitch and trim as shown in **Fig. 5**; press open to make **Unit 10-C**. Make 6 Unit 10-C's.

   In the same manner, use **squares N** and **S** and **rectangles T** to make 4 **Unit 10-D's**.

Fig. 5

Unit 10-C   Unit 10-D
(make 6)   (make 4)

5. In the same manner, use **squares N** and **U** and **rectangles V** to make 6 **Unit 11-C's**.

   In the same manner, use **squares N** and **U** and **rectangles V** to make 4 **Unit 11-D's**.

Unit 11-C   Unit 11-D
(make 6)   (make 4)

6. In the same manner, use **squares S** and **rectangles T** to make 10 **Unit 12's**.

Unit 12 (make 10)

7. In the same manner, use **squares N** and **rectangles T** to make 10 **Unit 13's**.

Unit 13 (make 10)

8. Sew 1 **Unit 12** and 1 **Unit 11-C** together to make **Unit 14-C**. Make 6 Unit 14-C's.

    Sew 1 **Unit 12** and 1 **Unit 11-D** together to make **Unit 14-D**. Make 4 Unit 14-D's.

Unit 14-C
(make 6)

Unit 14-D
(make 4)

9. Sew 1 **Unit 14-C** and 1 **Unit 10-C** together to make **Unit 15-C**. Make 6 Unit 15-C's.

    Sew 1 **Unit 14-D** and 1 **Unit 10-D** together to make **Unit 15-D**. Make 4 Unit 15-D's.

Unit 15-C
(make 6)

Unit 15-D
(make 4)

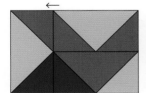 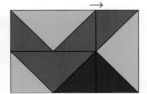

10. Sew 1 **Unit 13** and 1 **Triangle-Square** together to make **Unit 16-C**. Make 6 Unit 16-C's.

Sew 1 **Unit 13** and 1 **Triangle-Square** together to make **Unit 16-D**. Make 4 Unit 16-D's.

Unit 16-C
(make 6)

Unit 16-D
(make 4)

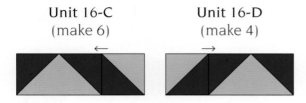

11. Sew 1 **Unit 15-C** and 1 **Unit 16-C** together to make **Block C**. Block C should measure 12½" x 12½" including seam allowances. Make 6 Block C's. Press seam allowances to one side.

Sew 1 **Unit 15-D** and 1 **Unit 16-D** together to make **Block D**. Block D should measure 12½" x 12½" including seam allowances. Make 4 Block D's. Press seam allowances to one side.

Block C
(make 6)

Block D
(make 4)

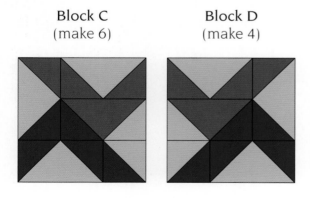

ASSEMBLING THE QUILT TOP CENTER

Pay special attention to Block placement and orientation when assembling the quilt top center.

1. Sew 1 **Block A**, 1 **Block B**, and 2 **Block C's** together to make **Row 1**. Repeat to make **Row 5**.

Rows 1 and 5

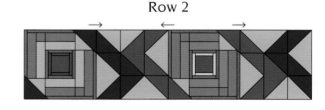

2. Sew 1 **Block A**, 1 **Block B**, and 2 **Block D's** together to make **Row 2**.

Row 2

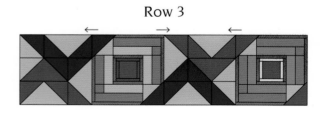

3. Sew 1 **Block A**, 1 **Block B**, and 2 **Block C's** together to make **Row 3**.

Row 3

4. Sew 1 **Block A**, 1 **Block B**, and 2 **Block D's** together to make **Row 4**.

Row 4

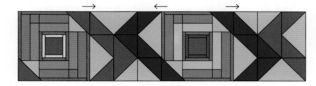

5. Referring to **Quilt Top Diagram**, sew **Rows** together to complete quilt top center.

ADDING THE BORDERS

1. Sew **inner border strips** together, end to end, to make 1 continuous strip.
2. To determine length of side inner borders, measure *length* across center of quilt top center. Cut 2 **side inner borders** from continuous strip. Matching centers and corners, sew side inner borders to quilt top center.
3. To determine length of top/bottom inner borders, measure *width* across center of quilt top center (including added borders). Cut 2 **top/bottom inner borders** from continuous strip. Matching centers and corners, sew top/bottom inner borders to quilt top center.
4. In the same manner, use **outer borders strips** to add **side** and then **top/bottom outer borders** to quilt top.

COMPLETING THE QUILT

1. Follow **Quilting**, page 56, to mark, layer, and quilt as desired. Quilt shown is machine quilted with a continuous curlicue pattern.
2. Follow **Making a Hanging Sleeve**, page 60, if a hanging sleeve is desired.
3. Use **binding strips** and follow **Binding**, page 60, to bind quilt.

Quilt Top Diagram

ROCKY ROAD

Finished Quilt Size: 60¾" x 75¾" (154 cm x 192 cm)
Finished Block Size: 15" x 15" (38 cm x 38 cm)

WHAT YOU WILL NEED

Yardage is based on 43"/44" (109 cm/112 cm) wide fabric
with a usable width of 40" (102 cm).

  1⅝ yds (1.5 m) of dark grey print fabric
  ¾ yd (69 cm) of light grey print fabric
  ¾ yd (69 cm) of black print fabric
  ¾ yd (69 cm) of black/magenta print fabric
  ¼ yd (23 cm) of magenta print fabric
  ¾ yd (69 cm) of cream large print fabric
  ⅜ yd (34 cm) of cream medium print fabric
  ⅝ yd (57 cm) of diagonal stripe print fabric
    for binding
  4¾ yds (4.3 m) of fabric for backing
You will also need:
  69" x 84" (175 cm x 213 cm) piece of batting

31

CUTTING THE PIECES

Follow **Rotary Cutting**, *page 54, to cut fabric. Cut all strips from the selvage-to-selvage width of the fabric. All measurements include* 1/4" *seam allowances.*

From dark grey print fabric:
- Cut 7 outer border strips 6" wide.
- Cut 2 wide strips 5 1/2" wide.

From light grey print fabric:
- Cut 2 wide strips 5 1/2" wide.
- Cut 4 narrow strips 3" wide.

From black print fabric:
- Cut 2 wide strips 5 1/2" wide.
- Cut 4 narrow strips 3" wide.

From black/magenta print fabric:
- Cut 6 inner border strips 2 1/2" wide.
- Cut 2 narrow strips 3" wide.

From magenta print fabric:
- Cut 2 narrow strips 3" wide.

From cream large print fabric:
- Cut 4 wide strips 5 1/2" wide.

From cream medium print fabric:
- Cut 2 wide strips 5 1/2" wide.

From diagonal stripe print fabric for binding:
- Cut 8 binding strips 2 1/4" wide.

MAKING THE BLOCK A'S

Follow **Piecing**, *page 55, and* **Pressing**, *page 56, to make quilt top.*

1. Sew 1 light grey **wide strip** and 1 black/magenta **narrow strip** together to make **Strip Set A**. Press seam allowances to narrow strip. Make 2 Strip Set A's. Cut across Strip Set A's at 3" intervals to make 24 **Unit 1's**.

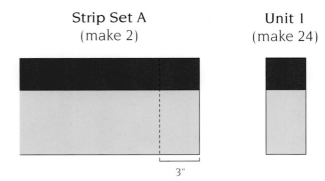

Strip Set A
(make 2)

3"

Unit 1
(make 24)

2. Sew 1 dark grey **wide strip** and 1 light grey **narrow strip** together to make **Strip Set B**. Press seam allowances to wide strip. Make 2 Strip Set B's. Cut across Strip Set B's at 5 1/2" intervals to make 12 **Unit 2's**.

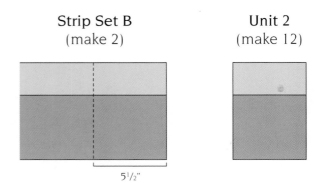

Strip Set B
(make 2)

5 1/2"

Unit 2
(make 12)

3. Sew 1 cream large print **wide strip** and 1 light grey **narrow strip** together to make **Strip Set C**. Press seam allowances to wide strip. Make 2 Strip Set C's. Cut across Strip Set C's at 5½" intervals to make 12 **Unit 3's**.

Strip Set C
(make 2)

Unit 3
(make 12)

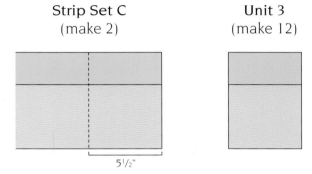

5½"

4. Sew 1 **Unit 1** and 1 **Unit 2** together to make **Unit 4**. Refer to **Pressing Tip** to press seam allowances. Unit 4 should measure 8" x 8" including seam allowances. Make 12 Unit 4's.

Unit 4
(make 12)

5. Sew 1 **Unit 1** and 1 **Unit 3** together to make **Unit 5**. Unit 5 should measure 8" x 8" including seam allowances. Make 12 Unit 5's.

Unit 5
(make 12)

6. Sew 1 **Unit 4** and 1 **Unit 5** together to make **Unit 6**. Press seam allowances to Unit 4. Make 12 Unit 6's.

Unit 6
(make 12)

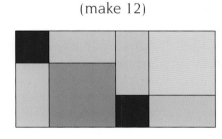

PRESSING TIP

*When pressing where 2 seams intersect, follow this tip to reduce bulk. Use a seam ripper to remove the stitches that are in the seams just made (**Fig. 1**). Press seam allowances in a circular motion. At the seam intersection, press the seam allowances open so that the center lies flat (**Fig. 2**).*

Fig 1

Fig. 2

7. Sew 2 **Unit 6's** together to make **Block A**. Block A should measure 15½" x 15½" including seam allowances. Make 6 Block A's.

Block A
(make 6)

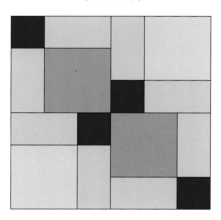

MAKING THE BLOCK B'S

1. Sew 1 black **wide strip** and 1 magenta **narrow strip** together to make **Strip Set D**. Press seam allowances to wide strip. Make 2 Strip Set D's. Cut across Strip Set D's at 3" intervals to make 24 **Unit 7's**.

Strip Set D   **Unit 7**
(make 2)   (make 24)

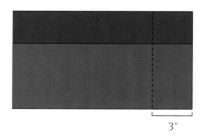

3"

2. Sew 1 cream medium print **wide strip** and 1 black **narrow strip** together to make **Strip Set E**. Press seam allowances to narrow strip. Make 2 Strip Set E's. Cut across Strip Set E's at 5½" intervals to make 12 **Unit 8's**.

Strip Set E   **Unit 8**
(make 2)   (make 12)

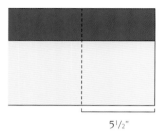

5½"

3. Sew 1 cream large print **wide strip** and 1 black **narrow strip** together to make **Strip Set F**. Press seam allowances to narrow strip. Make 2 Strip Set F's. Cut across Strip Set F's at 5½" intervals to make 12 **Unit 9's**.

Strip Set F   **Unit 9**
(make 2)   (make 12)

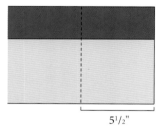

5½"

4. Sew 1 **Unit 7** and 1 **Unit 8** together to make **Unit 10**. Refer to **Pressing Tip** to press seam allowances. Unit 10 should measure 8" x 8" including seam allowances. Make 12 Unit 10's.

Unit 10
(make 12)

5. Sew 1 **Unit 7** and 1 **Unit 9** together to make **Unit 11**. Unit 11 should measure 8" x 8" including seam allowances. Make 12 Unit 11's.

Unit 11
(make 12)

6. Sew 1 **Unit 10** and 1 **Unit 11** together to make **Unit 12**. Press seam allowances to Unit 11. Make 12 Unit 12's.

Unit 12
(make 12)

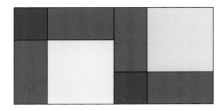

7. Sew 2 **Unit 12's** together to make **Block B**. Block B should measure $15^1/_2$" x $15^1/_2$" including seam allowances. Make 6 Block B's.

Block B
(make 6)

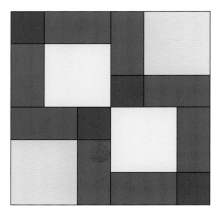

ASSEMBLING THE QUILT TOP CENTER

*Refer to **Quilt Top Diagram** to assemble quilt top.*

1. Sew 2 **Block A's** and 1 **Block B** together to make **Row A**. Press seam allowances to Block B. Make 2 Row A's.
2. Sew 2 **Block B's** and 1 **Block A** together to make **Row B**. Press seam allowances to Block B's. Make 2 Row B's.
3. Sew **Rows** together to complete quilt top center.

ADDING THE BORDERS

1. Sew **inner border strips** together, end to end, to make 1 continuous strip.
2. To determine length of side inner borders, measure *length* across center of quilt top center. Cut 2 **side inner borders** from continuous strip. Matching centers and corners, sew side inner borders to quilt top center.
3. To determine length of top/bottom inner borders, measure *width* across center of quilt top center (including added borders). Cut 2 **top/bottom inner borders** from continuous strip. Matching centers and corners, sew top/bottom inner borders to quilt top center.
4. In the same manner, use **outer borders strips** to add **side** and then **top/bottom outer borders** to quilt top.

COMPLETING THE QUILT

1. Follow **Quilting**, page 56, to mark, layer, and quilt as desired. Quilt shown is machine quilted with an all-over leaf pattern.
2. Follow **Making a Hanging Sleeve**, page 60, if a hanging sleeve is desired.
3. Use **binding strips** and follow **Binding**, page 60, to bind quilt.

Quilt Top Diagram

STAINED GLASS GARDEN

Finished Quilt Size: 63³/₄" x 81³/₄" (162 cm x 208 cm)

WHAT YOU WILL NEED

Yardage is based on 43"/44" (109 cm/112 cm) wide fabric with a usable width of 40" (102 cm).

    1¹/₂ yds (1.4 m) of multi-color/black mottled print fabric
    ³/₈ yd (34 cm) of pale multi-color mottled print fabric
    ¹/₂ yd (46 cm) of lavender mottled print fabric
    ¹/₂ yd (46 cm) of purple mottled print fabric
    ¹/₂ yd (46 cm) of medium multi-color mottled print fabric
    ⁵/₈ yd (57 cm) of green mottled print fabric
    ³/₈ yd (34 cm) of multi-color leopard print fabric
    3 yds (2.7 m) of black solid fabric (includes binding)
    5 yds (4.6 m) of fabric for backing

You will also need:

    72" x 90" (183 cm x 229 cm) piece of batting

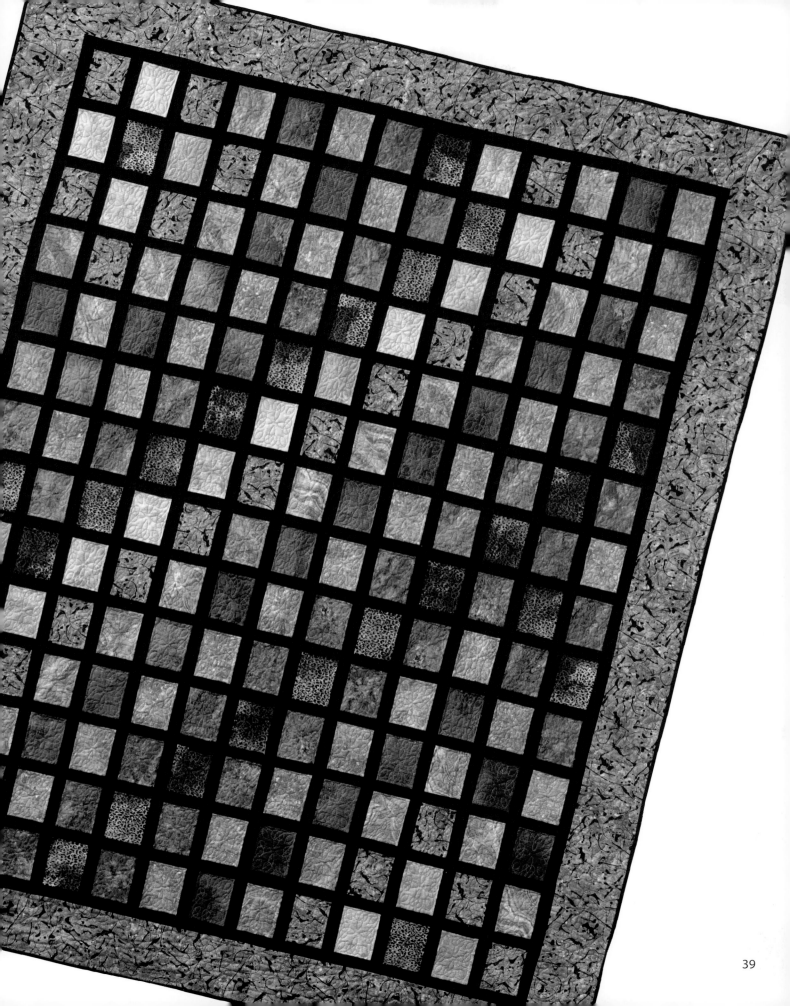

CUTTING THE PIECES

Follow **Rotary Cutting**, *page 54, to cut fabric. Cut all strips from the selvage-to-selvage width of the fabric. All measurements include ¼" seam allowances.*

From multi-color/black mottled print fabric:
- Cut 7 outer border strips 5½" wide.
- Cut 3 strips A 3½" wide.

From pale multi-color mottled print fabric:
- Cut 3 strips B 3½" wide.

From lavender mottled print fabric:
- Cut 4 strips C 3½" wide.

From purple mottled print fabric:
- Cut 4 strips D 3½" wide.

From medium multi-color mottled print fabric:
- Cut 4 strips E 3½" wide.

From green mottled print fabric:
- Cut 5 strips F 3½" wide.

From multi-color leopard print fabric:
- Cut 3 strips G 3½" wide.

From black solid fabric:
- Cut 7 inner border strips 1½" wide.
- Cut 18 sashing strips 1½" wide.
- Cut 26 strips H 1½" wide.
- Cut 8 binding strips 2¼" wide.

MAKING THE UNITS

Follow **Piecing**, *page 55, and* **Pressing**, *page 56, to make quilt top.*

1. Sew 1 **strip A** and 1 **strip H** together to make **Strip Set A**. Press seam allowances to strip H. Make 3 Strip Set A's. Cut across Strip Set A's at 4½" intervals to make 23 **Unit A's**.

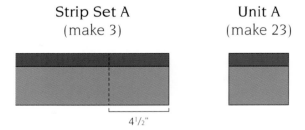

Strip Set A
(make 3)

Unit A
(make 23)

4½"

2. Sew 1 **strip B** and 1 **strip H** together to make **Strip Set B**. Press seam allowances to strip H. Make 3 Strip Set B's. Cut across Strip Set B's at 4½" intervals to make 18 **Unit B's**.

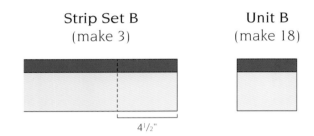

Strip Set B
(make 3)

Unit B
(make 18)

4½"

3. Sew 1 **strip C** and 1 **strip H** together to make **Strip Set C**. Press seam allowances to strip H. Make 4 Strip Set C's. Cut across Strip Set C's at 4½" intervals to make 25 **Unit C's**.

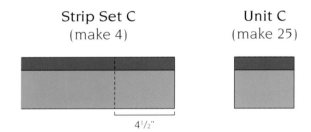

Strip Set C
(make 4)

Unit C
(make 25)

4½"

4. Sew 1 **strip D** and 1 **strip H** together to make **Strip Set D**. Press seam allowances to strip H. Make 4 Strip Set D's. Cut across Strip Set D's at 4½" intervals to make 28 **Unit D's**.

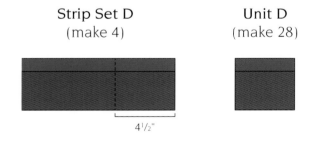

Strip Set D
(make 4)

Unit D
(make 28)

4½"

5. Sew 1 **strip E** and 1 **strip H** together to make **Strip Set E**. Press seam allowances to strip H. Make 4 Strip Set E's. Cut across Strip Set E's at $4^{1}/_{2}$" intervals to make 31 **Unit E's**.

Strip Set E	Unit E
(make 4)	(make 31)

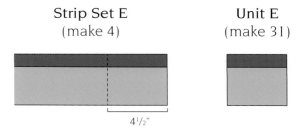

6. Sew 1 **strip F** and 1 **strip H** together to make **Strip Set F**. Press seam allowances to strip H. Make 5 Strip Set F's. Cut across Strip Set F's at $4^{1}/_{2}$" intervals to make 33 **Unit F's**.

Strip Set F	Unit F
(make 5)	(make 33)

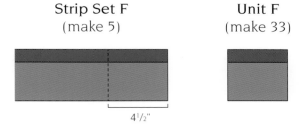

7. Sew 1 **strip G** and 1 **strip H** together to make **Strip Set G**. Press seam allowances to strip H. Make 3 Strip Set G's. Cut across Strip Set G's at $4^{1}/_{2}$" intervals to make 24 **Unit G's**.

Strip Set G	Unit G
(make 3)	(make 24)

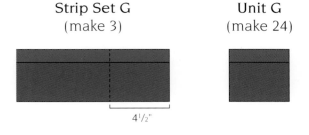

Placement Diagram

1	A	B	A	C	D	E	F	G	B	A	C	D	E
2	B	G	B	A	C	D	E	F	G	B	A	C	D
3	A	B	A	C	D	E	F	G	B	A	C	D	E
4	C	A	C	D	E	F	G	B	A	C	D	E	F
5	D	C	D	E	F	G	B	A	C	D	E	F	G
6	E	D	E	F	G	B	A	C	D	E	F	G	F
7	F	E	F	G	B	A	C	D	E	F	G	F	E
8	G	F	G	B	A	C	D	E	F	G	F	G	F
9	B	G	B	A	C	D	E	F	G	F	E	F	G
10	A	B	A	C	D	E	F	G	F	E	D	E	F
11	C	A	C	D	E	F	G	F	E	D	C	D	E
12	D	C	D	E	F	G	F	E	D	C	A	C	D
13	E	D	E	F	G	F	E	D	C	A	B	A	C
14	F	E	F	G	F	E	D	C	A	B	G	B	A

ASSEMBLING THE QUILT TOP CENTER

*Refer to **Placement Diagram** to make Rows.*

1. Sew 13 **Units** together to make **Row 1**. Using a seam ripper, remove black strip from right end of Row 1 (**Fig. 1**). Press seam allowances to black strips. Row 1 should measure $51\frac{1}{2}$" x $4\frac{1}{2}$". Write "Row 1" on a small piece of paper and pin paper to left end of completed Row.

Fig. 1

2. In the same manner, make **Rows 2-14**, labeling each Row as it is completed. Each Row should measure $51\frac{1}{2}$" x $4\frac{1}{2}$".
3. Sew **sashing strips** together, end to end, to make 1 continuous strip. From this strip, cut 13 **horizontal sashings** $51\frac{1}{2}$" long.
4. Referring to **Quilt Top Diagram**, sew **Rows** and **horizontal sashings** together to make quilt top center.

ADDING THE BORDERS

1. Sew **inner border strips** together, end to end, to make 1 continuous strip.
2. To determine length of side inner borders, measure *length* across center of quilt top center. Cut 2 **side inner borders** from continuous strip. Matching centers and corners, sew side inner borders to quilt top center.
3. To determine length of top/bottom inner borders, measure *width* across center of quilt top center (including added borders). Cut 2 **top/bottom inner borders** from continuous strip. Matching centers and corners, sew top/bottom inner borders to quilt top center.
4. In the same manner, use **outer borders strips** to add **side** and then **top/bottom outer borders** to quilt top.

COMPLETING THE QUILT

1. Follow **Quilting**, page 56, to mark, layer, and quilt as desired. Quilt shown is machine quilted with a loop pattern in the borders and sashings. A loop design is quilted in each print rectangle between the sashings.
2. Follow **Making a Hanging Sleeve**, page 60, if a hanging sleeve is desired.
3. Use **binding strips** and follow **Binding**, page 60, to bind quilt.

Quilt Top Diagram

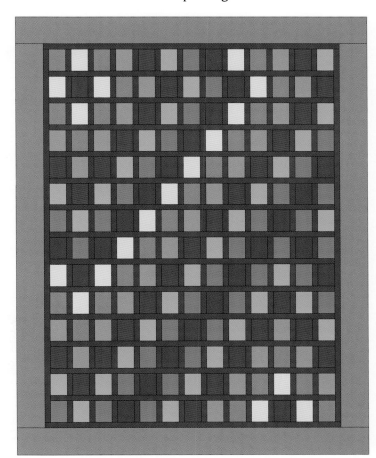

WOODS & WATER

Finished Quilt Size: 88³/₄" x 96³/₄" (225 cm x 246 cm)
Finished Block Size: 12" x 16" (30 cm x 41 cm)

WHAT YOU WILL NEED

Yardage is based on 43"/44" (109 cm/112 cm) wide fabric with a usable width of 40" (102 cm).

 2¹/₄ yds (2.1 m) of green/blue stripe fabric
 ¹/₂ yd (46 cm) of navy print fabric
 ⁵/₈ yd (57 cm) of light green print fabric
 1 yd (91 cm) of medium green print fabric
 2¹/₄ yds (2.1 m) of dark green print fabric
 ⁷/₈ yd (80 cm) of light blue print fabric
 1¹/₈ yds (1 m) of medium blue print fabric
 1³/₄ yds (1.6 m) of dark blue print fabric
 ⁷/₈ yd (80 cm) of fabric for binding
 8¹/₈ yds (7.4 m) of fabric for backing

You will also need:

 97" x 105" (246 cm x 267 cm) piece of batting

CUTTING THE PIECES

Follow **Rotary Cutting**, *page 54, to cut fabric. Cut all strips from the selvage-to-selvage width of the fabric. All measurements include* ¹/₄" *seam allowances.*

From green/blue stripe fabric:
- Cut 11 **outer border strips** 6¹/₂" wide.

From navy print fabric:
- Cut 4 strips 3¹/₂" wide. From these strips, cut 30 **rectangles A** 3¹/₂" x 4¹/₂".

From light green print fabric:
- Cut 3 strips 2¹/₂" wide. From these strips, cut 30 **strips B** 2¹/₂" x 3¹/₂".
- Cut 5 strips 2" wide. From these strips, cut 30 **strips C** 2" x 6¹/₂".

From medium green print fabric:
- Cut 5 strips 2¹/₂" wide. From these strips, cut 30 **strips F** 2¹/₂" x 6¹/₂".
- Cut 10 strips 2" wide. From these strips, cut 30 **strips G** 2" x 10¹/₂".

From dark green print fabric:
- Cut 9 **inner border strips** 2¹/₂" wide.
- Cut 8 strips 2¹/₂" wide. From these strips, cut 30 **strips J** 2¹/₂" x 9¹/₂".
- Cut 15 strips 2" wide. From these strips, cut 30 **strips K** 2" x 14¹/₂".

From light blue print fabric:
- Cut 4 strips 2¹/₂" wide. From these strips, cut 30 **strips D** 2¹/₂" x 5".
- Cut 8 strips 2" wide. From these strips, cut 30 **strips E** 2" x 8¹/₂".

From medium blue print fabric:
- Cut 6 strips 2¹/₂" wide. From these strips, cut 30 **strips H** 2¹/₂" x 8".
- Cut 10 strips 2" wide. From these strips, cut 30 **strips I** 2" x 12¹/₂".

From dark blue print fabric:
- Cut 10 strips 2¹/₂" wide. From these strips, cut 30 **strips L** 2¹/₂" x 11".
- Cut 15 strips 2" wide. From these strips, cut 30 **strips M** 2" x 16¹/₂".

From fabric for binding:
- Cut 11 **binding strips** 2¹/₄" wide.

MAKING THE BLOCK A'S

Follow **Piecing**, *page 55, and* **Pressing**, *page 56, to make quilt top.*

1. Sew 1 **rectangle A** and 1 **strip B** together to make **Unit 1**. Press seam allowances to strip B. Make 16 Unit 1's.

Unit 1 (make 16)

2. Sew 1 **Unit 1** and 1 **strip C** together to make **Unit 2**. Press seam allowances to strip C. Make 16 Unit 2's.

Unit 2 (make 16)

3. Sew 1 **Unit 2** and 1 **strip D** together to make **Unit 3**. Press seam allowances to strip D. Make 16 Unit 3's.

Unit 3 (make 16)

4. Sew 1 **Unit 3** and 1 **strip E** together to make **Unit 4**. Press seam allowances to strip E. Make 16 Unit 4's.

Unit 4 (make 16)

5. Continue in the same manner, working *counter clockwise*, to add **strips F-M** to make **Block A**. Always press seam allowances to strip just added. Block A should measure 12½" x 16½" including seam allowances. Make 16 Block A's.

Block A (make 16)

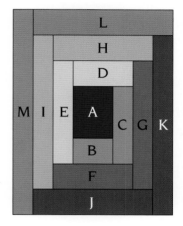

MAKING THE BLOCK B'S

1. Sew 1 **rectangle A** and 1 **strip B** together to make **Unit 5**. Press seam allowances to strip B. Make 14 Unit 5's.

Unit 5 (make 14)

2. Sew 1 **Unit** 5 and 1 **strip C** together to make
    Unit 6. Press seam allowances to strip C. Make
    14 Unit 6's.

    Unit 6 (make 14)

3. Sew 1 **Unit** 6 and 1 **strip D** together to make
    Unit 7. Press seam allowances to strip D. Make
    14 Unit 7's.

    Unit 7 (make 14)

4. Sew 1 **Unit** 7 and 1 **strip E** together to make
    Unit 8. Press seam allowances to strip E. Make
    14 Unit 8's.

    Unit 8 (make 14)

    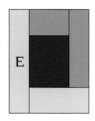

5. Continue in the same manner, working
    clockwise, to add **strips F-M** to make **Block B**.
    Always press seam allowances to strip just
    added. Block B should measure 12½" x 16½"
    including seam allowances. Make 14 Block B's.

    Block B (make 14)

    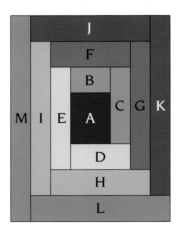

ASSEMBLING THE QUILT TOP CENTER

1. Sew 2 **Block A's** and 4 **Block B's** together to
    make **Row 1**. Press seam allowances in one
    direction.

    Row 1

    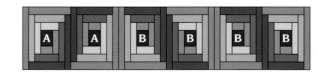

2. Sew 2 **Block A's** and 4 **Block B's** together to make **Row 2**. Press seam allowances in the opposite direction of Row 1.

Row 2

3. Sew 4 **Block A's** and 2 **Block B's** together to make **Row 3**. Press seam allowances in the same direction as Row 1. Repeat to make **Row 5**.

Rows 3 and 5

4. Sew 4 **Block A's** and 2 **Block B's** together to make **Row 4**. Press seam allowances in the same direction as Row 2.

Row 4

5. Referring to **Quilt Top Diagram**, sew **Rows** together to complete quilt top center.

ADDING THE INNER BORDER

1. Sew **inner border strips** together, end to end, to make 1 continuous strip.
2. To determine length of side inner borders, measure *length* across center of quilt top center. Cut 2 **side inner borders** from continuous strip. Matching centers and corners, sew side inner borders to quilt top center.
3. To determine length of top/bottom inner borders, measure *width* across center of quilt top center (including added borders). Cut 2 **top/bottom inner borders** from continuous strip. Matching centers and corners, sew top/bottom inner borders to quilt top.

ADDING THE OUTER BORDER

1. Sew **outer border strips** together, end to end, to make 1 continuous strip.
2. Measure *width* across center of quilt top and add 16". Cut 2 **top/bottom outer borders** the determined measurement from continuous strip. Do not add borders to quilt top at this time.
3. Measure *length* across center of quilt top and add 16". Cut 2 **side outer borders** the determined measurement from continuous strip. Do not add borders to quilt top at this time.

Quilt Top Diagram

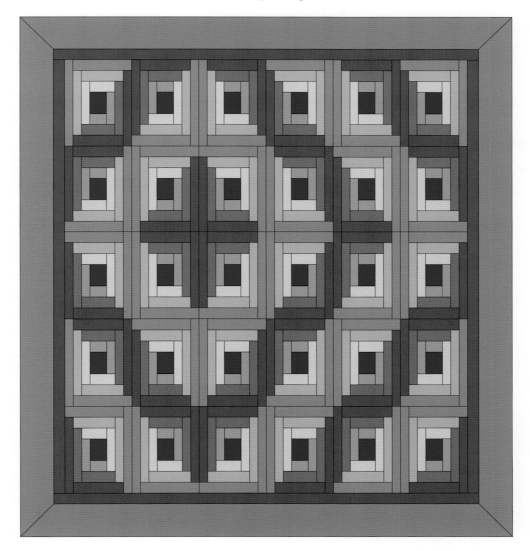

4. Mark the center of each edge of quilt top. Mark the center of 1 long edge of **top outer border**. Matching center marks and raw edges, pin border to center of quilt top edge. From center of border, measure out ¹/₂ the width of the quilt top in both directions and mark. Match marks on border with corners of quilt top and pin. Pin border to quilt top between center and corners. Sew border to quilt top, beginning and ending seams exactly ¹/₄" from each corner of quilt top and backstitching at beginning and end of stitching (**Fig. 1**).

Fig. 1

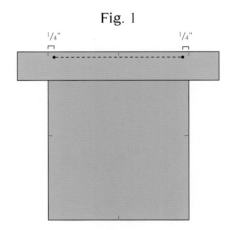

5. Repeat Step 4 to sew **bottom**, then **side outer borders** to quilt top. To temporarily move top/bottom outer borders out of the way, fold and pin ends as shown in **Fig. 2**.

Fig. 2

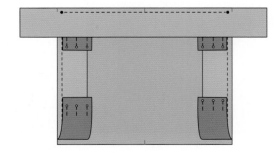

6. Fold 1 corner of quilt top diagonally with right sides together; use rotary cutting ruler to mark stitching line as shown in **Fig. 3**. Pin borders together along drawn line. Sew on drawn line, backstitching at beginning and end of stitching (**Fig. 4**).

Fig. 3

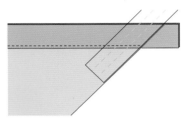

Fig. 4

7. Turn mitered corner right side up. Check to see that there is not a gap at the inner end of the seam and that the corner does not pucker.
8. Trim seam allowances to ¹/₄"; press to 1 side.
9. Repeat Steps 6-8 to miter each remaining corner.

COMPLETING THE QUILT

1. Follow **Quilting**, page 56, to mark, layer, and quilt as desired. Quilt shown is machine quilted with an all-over pattern of overlapping circles.
2. Follow **Making a Hanging Sleeve**, page 60, if a hanging sleeve is desired.
3. Use **binding strips** and follow **Binding**, page 60, to bind quilt.

GENERAL INSTRUCTIONS

To make your quilting easier and more enjoyable, we encourage you to carefully read all of the general instructions, study the color photographs, and familiarize yourself with the individual project instructions before beginning a project.

FABRICS

SELECTING FABRICS
Choose high-quality, medium-weight 100% cotton fabrics. All-cotton fabrics hold a crease better, fray less, and are easier to quilt than cotton/polyester blends.

Yardage requirements listed for each project are based on 43"/44" wide fabric with a "usable" width of 40" after shrinkage and trimming selvages. Actual usable width will probably vary slightly from fabric to fabric. Our recommended yardage lengths should be adequate for occasional re-squaring of fabric when many cuts are required.

PREPARING FABRICS
We recommend that all fabrics be washed, dried, and pressed before cutting. If fabrics are not pre-washed, washing the finished quilt will cause shrinkage and give it a more "antiqued" look and feel. Bright and dark colors, which may run, should always be washed before cutting. After washing and drying fabric, fold lengthwise with wrong sides together and matching selvages.

ROTARY CUTTING

- Place fabric on work surface with fold closest to you.

- Cut all strips from the selvage-to-selvage width of the fabric unless otherwise indicated in project instructions.

- Square left edge of fabric using rotary cutter and rulers (**Figs.** 1-2).

Fig. 2

Fig. 1

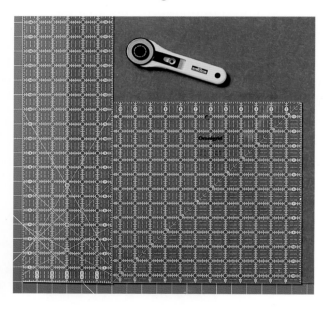

- To cut each strip required for a project, place ruler over cut edge of fabric, aligning desired marking on ruler with cut edge; make cut (**Fig.** 3).

Fig. 3

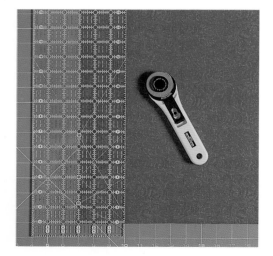

- When cutting several strips from a single piece of fabric, it is important to make sure that cuts remain at a perfect right angle to the fold; square fabric as needed.

PIECING

Precise cutting, followed by accurate piecing, will ensure that all pieces of quilt top fit together well.

- Set sewing machine stitch length for approximately 11 stitches per inch.

- Use neutral-colored general-purpose sewing thread (not quilting thread) in needle and in bobbin.

- An accurate 1/4" seam allowance is *essential*. Presser feet that are 1/4" wide are available for most sewing machines.

- When piecing, always place pieces right sides together and match raw edges; pin if necessary.

- Chain piecing saves time and will usually result in more accurate piecing.

- Trim away points of seam allowances that extend beyond edges of sewn pieces.

SEWING ACROSS SEAM INTERSECTIONS

When sewing across intersection of two seams, place pieces right sides together and match seams exactly, making sure seam allowances are pressed in opposite directions (**Fig. 4**).

Fig. 4

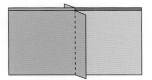

SEWING SHARP POINTS

To ensure sharp points when joining triangular or diagonal pieces, stitch across the center of the "X" (shown in pink) formed on wrong side by previous seams (**Fig. 5**).

Fig. 5

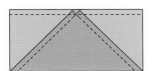

PRESSING

- Use steam iron set on "Cotton" for all pressing.

- Press after sewing each seam.

- Seam allowances are almost always pressed to one side, usually toward darker fabric. However, to reduce bulk it may occasionally be necessary to press seam allowances toward the lighter fabric or even to press them open.

- To prevent dark fabric seam allowance from showing through light fabric, trim darker seam allowance slightly narrower than lighter seam allowance.

- To press long seams, such as those in long strip sets, without curving or other distortion, lay strips across width of the ironing board.

QUILTING

*Quilting holds the three layers (top, batting, and backing) of the quilt together and can be done by hand or machine. Because marking, layering, and quilting are interrelated and may be done in different orders depending on circumstances, please read entire **Quilting** section, pages 56-59, before beginning project.*

TYPES OF QUILTING DESIGNS

In the Ditch Quilting
Quilting along seamlines or along edges of appliquéd pieces is called "in the ditch" quilting. This type of quilting should be done on side **opposite** seam allowance and does not have to be marked.

Outline Quilting
Quilting a consistent distance, usually $1/4$", from seam or appliqué is called "outline" quilting. Outline quilting may be marked, or $1/4$" wide masking tape may be placed along seamlines for quilting guide. (Do not leave tape on quilt longer than necessary, since it may leave an adhesive residue.)

Motif Quilting
Quilting a design, such as a feathered wreath, is called "motif" quilting. This type of quilting should be marked before basting quilt layers together.

Echo Quilting
Quilting that follows the outline of an appliquéd or pieced design with two or more parallel lines is called "echo" quilting. This type of quilting does not need to be marked.

Channel Quilting
Quilting with straight, parallel lines is called "channel" quilting. This type of quilting may be marked or stitched using a guide.

Crosshatch Quilting
Quilting straight lines in a grid pattern is called "crosshatch" quilting. Lines may be stitched parallel to edges of quilt or stitched diagonally. This type of quilting may be marked or stitched using a guide.

Meandering Quilting

Quilting in random curved lines and swirls is called "meandering" quilting. Quilting lines should not cross or touch each other. This type of quilting does not need to be marked.

Stipple Quilting

Meandering quilting that is very closely spaced is called "stipple" quilting. Stippling will flatten the area quilted and is often stitched in background areas to raise appliquéd or pieced designs. This type of quilting does not need to be marked.

MARKING QUILTING LINES

Quilting lines may be marked using fabric marking pencils, chalk markers, or water- or air-soluble pens.

Simple quilting designs may be marked with chalk or chalk pencil after basting. A small area may be marked, then quilted, before moving to next area to be marked. Intricate designs should be marked before basting using a more durable marker.

Caution: Pressing may permanently set some marks. **Test** different markers **on scrap fabric** to find one that marks clearly and can be thoroughly removed.

A wide variety of pre-cut quilting stencils, as well as entire books of quilting patterns, are available. Using a stencil makes it easier to mark intricate or repetitive designs.

To make a stencil from a pattern, center template plastic over pattern and use a permanent marker to trace pattern onto plastic. Use a craft knife with single or double blade to cut channels along traced lines (**Fig. 6**).

Fig. 6

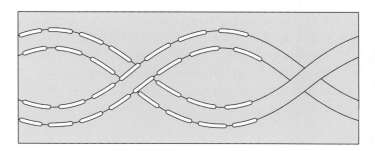

PREPARING THE BACKING

To allow for slight shifting of quilt top during quilting, backing should be approximately 4" larger on all sides. Yardage requirements listed for quilt backings are calculated for 43"/44" wide fabric. Using 90" wide or 108" wide fabric for the backing of a bed-sized quilt may eliminate piecing. To piece a backing using 43"/44" wide fabric, use the following instructions.

1. Measure length and width of quilt top; add 8" to each measurement.

2. If determined width is 79" or less, cut backing fabric into two lengths the determined *length* measurement. Trim selvages. Place lengths with right sides facing and sew long edges together, forming a tube (**Fig. 7**). Match seams and press along one fold (**Fig. 8**). Cut along pressed fold to form a single piece (**Fig. 9**).

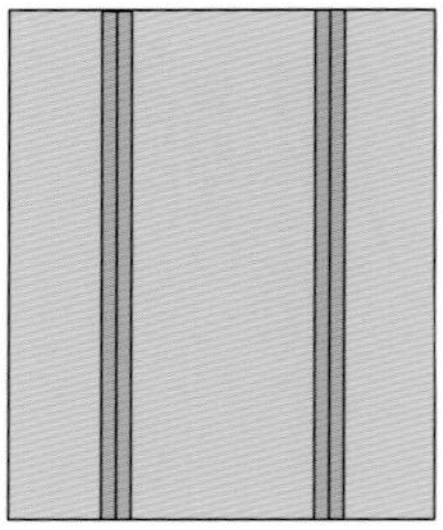

3. If determined width is more than 79", it may require less fabric yardage if the backing is pieced horizontally. Divide the determined *length* measurement by 40" to determine how many widths will be needed. Cut the required number of widths the determined *width* measurement. Trim selvages. Sew long edges together to form a single piece.

4. Trim backing to size determined in Step 1; press seam allowances open.

CHOOSING THE BATTING

The appropriate batting will make quilting easier. For fine hand quilting, choose low-loft batting. All cotton or cotton/polyester blend battings work well for machine quilting because the cotton helps "grip" quilt layers. If quilt is to be tied, a high-loft batting, sometimes called extra-loft or fat batting, may be used to make quilt "fluffy."

Types of batting include cotton, polyester, wool, cotton/polyester blend, cotton/wool blend, and silk.

When selecting batting, refer to package labels for characteristics and care instructions. Cut batting same size as prepared backing.

Fig. 7   Fig. 8

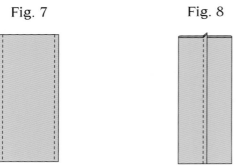

Fig. 9

ASSEMBLING THE QUILT

1. Examine wrong side of quilt top closely; trim any seam allowances and clip any threads that may show through front of the quilt. Press quilt top, being careful not to "set" any marked quilting lines.

2. Place backing *wrong* side up on flat surface. Use masking tape to tape edges of backing to surface. Place batting on top of backing fabric. Smooth batting gently, being careful not to stretch or tear. Center quilt top *right* side up on batting.

3. Use 1" rustproof safety pins to "pin-baste" all layers together, spacing pins approximately 4" apart. Begin at center and work toward outer edges to secure all layers. If possible, place pins away from areas that will be quilted, although pins may be removed as needed when quilting.

MACHINE QUILTING METHODS

Use general-purpose thread in bobbin. Do not use quilting thread. Thread the needle of the machine with general-purpose thread or transparent monofilament thread to make quilting blend with quilt top fabrics. Use decorative thread, such as a metallic or contrasting-color general-purpose thread, to make quilting lines stand out more.

Straight-Line Quilting

The term "straight-line" is somewhat deceptive, since curves (especially gentle ones) as well as straight lines can be stitched with this technique.

1. Set stitch length for six to ten stitches per inch and attach walking foot to sewing machine.

2. Determine which section of quilt will have the longest continuous quilting line, oftentimes the area from center top to center bottom. Roll up and secure each edge of quilt to help reduce the bulk, keeping fabrics smooth. Smaller projects may not need to be rolled.

3. Begin stitching on longest quilting line, using very short stitches for the first $\frac{1}{4}$" to "lock" quilting. Stitch across project, using one hand on each side of walking foot to slightly spread fabric and to guide fabric through machine. Lock stitches at end of quilting line.

4. Continue machine quilting, stitching longer quilting lines first to stabilize quilt before moving on to other areas.

Free-Motion Quilting

Free-motion quilting may be free form or may follow a marked pattern.

1. Attach darning foot to sewing machine and lower or cover feed dogs.

2. Position quilt under darning foot; lower foot. Holding top thread, take a stitch and pull bobbin thread to top of quilt. To "lock" beginning of quilting line, hold top and bobbin threads while making three to five stitches in place.

3. Use one hand on each side of darning foot to slightly spread fabric and to move fabric through the machine. Even stitch length is achieved by using smooth, flowing hand motion and steady machine speed. Slow machine speed and fast hand movement will create long stitches. Fast machine speed and slow hand movement will create short stitches. Move quilt sideways, back and forth, in a circular motion, or in a random motion to create desired designs; do not rotate quilt. Lock stitches at end of each quilting line.

MAKING A HANGING SLEEVE

Attaching a hanging sleeve to the back of a quilt before the binding is added will allow you to display the quilt on a wall.

1. Measure width of quilt top edge and subtract 1". Cut piece of fabric 7" wide by determined measurement.
2. Press short edges of fabric piece ¼" to wrong side; press edges ¼" to wrong side again and machine stitch in place.
3. Matching wrong sides, fold piece in half lengthwise to form a tube.
4. Follow project instructions to sew binding to quilt top and to trim backing and batting. Before Blindstitching binding to backing, match raw edges and stitch hanging sleeve to center top edge on back of quilt.
5. Finish binding quilt, treating hanging sleeve as part of backing.
6. Blindstitch bottom of hanging sleeve to backing, taking care not to stitch through to front of quilt.
7. Insert dowel or slat into hanging sleeve.

BINDING

1. Using diagonal seams (**Fig. 10**), sew binding strips called for in project together end to end.

Fig. 10

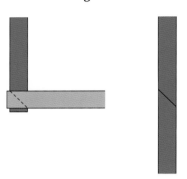

2. Matching wrong sides and raw edges, carefully press strip in half lengthwise to complete binding.
3. Beginning with one end near center on bottom edge of quilt, lay binding around quilt to make sure that seams in binding will not end up at a corner. Adjust placement if necessary. Matching raw edges of binding to raw edge of quilt top, pin binding to right side of quilt along one edge.
4. When you reach first corner, mark ¼" from corner of quilt top (**Fig. 11**).

Fig. 11

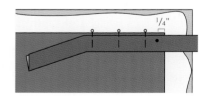

5. Beginning approximately 10" from end of binding and using ¼" seam allowance, sew binding to quilt, backstitching at beginning of stitching and at mark (**Fig.** 12). Lift needle out of fabric and clip thread.

Fig. 12

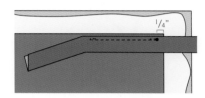

6. Fold binding as shown in **Figs.** 13-14 and pin binding to adjacent side, matching raw edges. When you've reached the next corner, mark ¼" from edge of quilt top.

Fig. 13

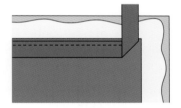

Fig. 14

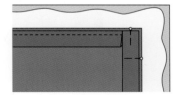

7. Backstitching at edge of quilt top, sew pinned binding to quilt (**Fig.** 15); backstitch at the next mark. Lift needle out of fabric and clip thread.

Fig. 15

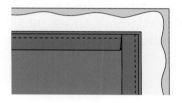

8. Continue sewing binding to quilt, stopping approximately 10" from starting point (**Fig.** 16).

Fig. 16

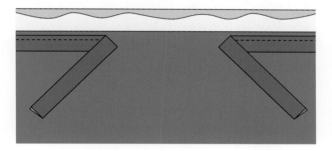

9. Bring beginning and end of binding to center of opening and fold each end back, leaving a ¼" space between folds (**Fig.** 17). Finger press folds.

Fig. 17

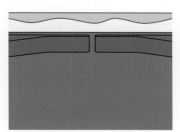

10. Unfold ends of binding and draw a line across wrong side in finger-pressed crease. Draw a line through the lengthwise pressed fold of binding at the same spot to create a cross mark. With edge of ruler at cross mark, line up 45° angle marking on ruler with one long side of binding. Draw a diagonal line from edge to edge. Repeat on remaining end, making sure that the two diagonal lines are angled the same way (**Fig. 18**).

Fig. 18

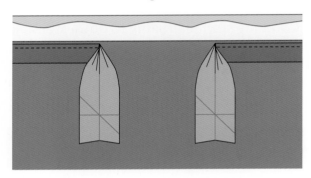

11. Matching right sides and diagonal lines, pin binding ends together at right angles (**Fig. 19**).

Fig. 19

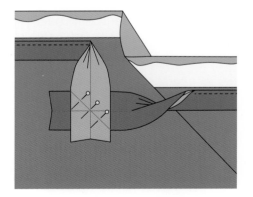

12. Machine stitch along diagonal line (**Fig. 20**), removing pins as you stitch.

Fig. 20

13. Lay binding against quilt to double check that it is correct length.
14. Trim binding ends, leaving 1/4" seam allowances; press seam allowances open. Stitch binding to quilt.
15. Trim backing and batting even with edges of quilt top.

16. On one edge of quilt, fold binding over to quilt backing and pin pressed edge in place, covering stitching line (**Fig. 21**). On adjacent side, fold binding over, forming a mitered corner (**Fig. 22**). Repeat to pin remainder of binding in place.

Fig. 21

Fig. 22

17. Blindstitch binding to backing, taking care not to stitch through to front of quilt. To blindstitch, come up at 1, go down at 2, and come up at 3 (**Fig. 23**).

Fig. 23

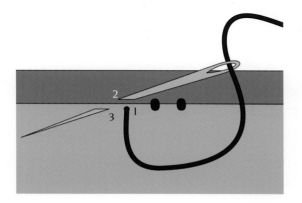

SIGNING AND DATING YOUR QUILT

A completed quilt is a work of art and should be signed and dated. There are many different ways to do this and numerous books on the subject. The label should reflect the style of the quilt, the occasion or person for which it was made, and the quilter's own particular talents. The following are suggestions for recording the history of the quilt or adding a sentiment for future generations.

- Embroider quilter's name, date, and any additional information on quilt top or backing. Matching floss, such as cream floss on white border, will leave a subtle record. Bright or contrasting floss will make the information stand out.

- Make label from muslin and use permanent marker to write information. Use different colored permanent markers to make label more decorative. Stitch label to back of quilt.

- Use photo-transfer paper to add image to white or cream fabric label. Stitch label to back of quilt.

- Piece an extra block from quilt top pattern to use as label. Add information with permanent fabric pen. Appliqué block to back of quilt.

Metric Conversion Chart

Inches x 2.54 = centimeters (cm)		Yards x .9144 = meters (m)
Inches x 25.4 = millimeters (mm)		Yards x 91.44 = centimeters (cm)
Inches x .0254 = meters (m)		Centimeters x .3937 = inches (")
		Meters x 1.0936 = yards (yd)

Standard Equivalents

1/8"	3.2 mm	0.32 cm	1/8 yard	11.43 cm	0.11 m
1/4"	6.35 mm	0.635 cm	1/4 yard	22.86 cm	0.23 m
3/8"	9.5 mm	0.95 cm	3/8 yard	34.29 cm	0.34 m
1/2"	12.7 mm	1.27 cm	1/2 yard	45.72 cm	0.46 m
5/8"	15.9 mm	1.59 cm	5/8 yard	57.15 cm	0.57 m
3/4"	19.1 mm	1.91 cm	3/4 yard	68.58 cm	0.69 m
7/8"	22.2 mm	2.22 cm	7/8 yard	80 cm	0.8 m
1 "	25.4 mm	2.54 cm	1 yard	91.44 cm	0.91 m

MEET THE DESIGNERS

SUE HARVEY AND SANDY BOOBAR are the owners of Pine Tree Country Quilts. Sue says, "We established the company seven years ago. The name was inspired by the fact that we each live in a grove of pine trees in the middle of Maine."

Sandy is a longarm machine quilter. Sue is a longtime quilter who helped develop a national quilting magazine in the 1990s. Sandy and Sue met when Sue needed to get some quilts finished. In 2005, they began working together on quilt designs, opening a fabric and kit shop in Stillwater, Maine. With 40 years of quilting experience between them, Sue and Sandy find the business to be a perfect fit. They regularly design quilts for magazines and fabric companies, and they sell their kits and patterns by phone and on their website at PineTreeCountryQuilts.com.

Special thanks to Fabri-Quilt, Red Rooster Fabrics, Northcott, Robert Kaufman, Bernatex, Fairfield, and Coats and Clark. Machine Quilting by Sandy's Hideaway Quilts.